little bee books

A division of Bonnier Publishing
853 Broadway, New York, New York 10003
Copyright © 2016 by Bonnier Publishing
All rights reserved, including the right of reproduction in whole or in part in any form.
LITTLE BEE BOOKS is a trademark of Bonnier Publishing Group, and associated colophon is a trademark of Bonnier Publishing Group.
Manufactured in the United States   LB 0516
First Edition 10 9 8 7 6 5 4 3 2 1

Library of Congress Cataloging-in-Publication Data:
Names: Ohlin, Nancy, author. | Larkum, Adam, illustrator.
Title: Blast Back! : The American Revolution / by Nancy Ohlin ; illustrated by Adam Larkum.
Other titles: American Revolution
Description: First edition. | New York : little bee books, 2016. | Series: Blast Back! |
Includes bibliographical references. | Audience: Ages 7–10 | Audience: Grades 4–6
Subjects: LCSH: United States—History—Revolution, 1775–1783—Juvenile literature.
Classification: LCC E208 .O35 2016 | DDC 973.3—dc23
LC record available at http://lccn.loc.gov/2015042798

Identifiers: LCCN 2015042798
ISBN 9781499801224 (pbk) | ISBN 9781499801231 (hc)

littlebeebooks.com
bonnierpublishing.com

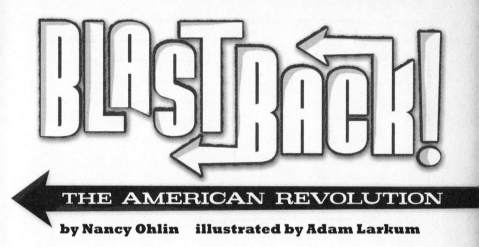

BLAST BACK!

THE AMERICAN REVOLUTION

by Nancy Ohlin   illustrated by Adam Larkum

little bee books

CONTENTS

Introduction

Have you ever heard people mention the American Revolution and wonder what they were talking about? What's a revolution? Is it the same thing as a war? Who was involved? And what was the outcome?

Let's blast back in time for a little adventure and find out. . . .

A Brief History of the American Revolution

You're wondering: What exactly is the American Revolution?

The word "revolution" comes from the Latin word *revolutio* ("turn around") and has different meanings. In this case, it means an effort by a group to "turn around" a government or social order through military action.

The American Revolution was a war between the United Kingdom of Great Britain and British citizens living in America. The citizens, or colonists, were unhappy with the way their mother country was treating them. (A mother country is the country where its colonists come from.) The war started in 1775 and lasted until 1783. It was fought on both land and sea.

In the beginning of the war, the colonists were just fighting for their rights, like the right to be represented in the British government and the right to trade freely. But after the first year, it turned into a fight for independence as the colonists decided to cut their ties to Britain completely. In 1776, they formed the United States of America.

In 1778, France joined the war on the side of the United States; so did Spain in 1779. Others became involved, too, including the Germans, the Dutch, and the Native Americans.

The American Revolution is also called the Revolutionary War, the American Revolutionary War, the War of Independence, and the United States War of Independence.

Britain by Any Other Name

At the time of the American Revolution, the United Kingdom of Great Britain was made up of England, Scotland, and Wales. Other names for this country are the United Kingdom, Great Britain, and Britain. Today, it includes Northern Ireland and is officially called the United Kingdom of Great Britain and Northern Ireland.

How the Thirteen Colonies Came to Be

In 1492 the Italian explorer Christopher Columbus made a sea voyage across the Atlantic Ocean to seek a shorter route to Asia. Asia had become a major source of spices, medicines, and other goods for Europeans to use, sell, and trade.

On October 12 of that year, Columbus reached an island that he thought was part of Asia. But the island, which he named San Salvador, was nowhere near Asia; instead, it was part of what later came to be called the Americas: North America (including Central America and the Caribbean islands) and South America.

Columbus's accidental discovery of the Americas opened up the way for European countries to expand their borders and grow their empires. Citizens of Britain, Spain, France, and other European countries moved to the so-called "New World" and settled there, usually to farm or set up

businesses. Many settlers were excited by the prospect of free or cheap land and bountiful natural resources. Others saw an opportunity to get rich by exporting goods back to Europe. And some came to practice their own religions freely without fear of being punished.

These settlements were governed by their mother countries in Europe. The first permanent British settlement was in Jamestown, Virginia, in 1607. Jamestown was named after King James I, who was then king of England. By 1732, there were thirteen British colonies up and down the Atlantic coast: Virginia, New York, Massachusetts, Maryland, Rhode Island, Connecticut, New Hampshire, Delaware, North Carolina, South Carolina, New Jersey, Pennsylvania, and Georgia. (Note that these places were still colonies, not states. Statehood didn't happen until much later.)

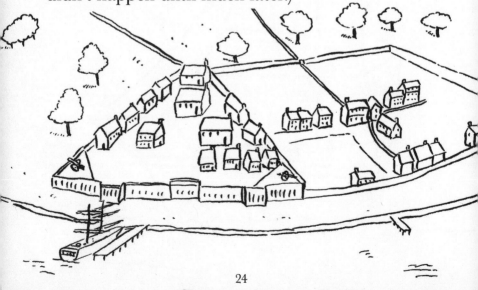

The thirteen colonies enjoyed a lot of independence. Even though they were under British rule, each colony had its own governor, appointed by the British king, and elected an assembly to deal with political matters. Also, Britain was three thousand miles away, across the Atlantic Ocean. The government was too busy with its own problems to pay attention to its distant charges in America.

But this changed after the French and Indian War.

25

Native Americans

Native Americans had been living in North America way before the European settlers arrived. Many lost their lives or lands as a result of colonization.

Many native people fought against the British in the French and Indian War. In the Revolutionary War, some continued to fight against the British, while some fought for the British.

The Iroquois Confederacy (also called the Six Nations) is a good example of this split in loyalties. During the Revolutionary War, two of the tribes allied with the Americans, and the other four allied with the British. After the war, the Iroquois signed a treaty that resulted in even more loss of land for them.

Taxation without Representation

The French and Indian War began in 1754. Britain went to war against France on American soil over who controlled which territories. The British had colonial troops on their side, including a young major named George Washington. (Yes, that George Washington!) The French had many Native American allies.

The French and Indian War finally ended in 1763 with a British victory. But the war had been long and expensive for the British, and they needed money to pay off their debts. They also wanted to take tighter control of their colonies in America and elsewhere to avoid more rebellion. ("Rebellion" means resisting or rising up against a government or other authority.)

One way to accomplish all this was through more taxation. (With taxation, a government makes its citizens pay money so it can, in turn, pay for its own expenses.) In 1765, Parliament, the law-making branch of the British government, passed a law called the Stamp Act. The Stamp Act imposed a tax in the form of British stamps that colonists had to buy for legal and business documents.

The Stamp Act was not the first effort by the British to tax the colonists. But the colonists objected to this tax law more strongly than the previous ones. For one thing, they had grown increasingly unhappy about "taxation without representation." If Parliament was going to tax them, they wanted their own members in Parliament to represent their interests.

The colonists' protests against the Stamp Act included riots and stamp burning. The British finally decided to repeal, or cancel, the law in 1766. But at the same time, Parliament issued the Declaratory Act, which stated that Parliament had the absolute right to create new tax and other laws for the colonies in "all cases whatsoever."

By this time the colonies were used to making decisions for themselves and governing themselves too. Britain wanted to put an end to all this independence by imposing even more restrictions.

Tensions between the two sides continued to worsen.

The Boston Massacre

The British had been sending more and more of their troops to the colonies since the end of the French and Indian War to keep order. Some of the colonists liked having the protection of the troops. But many resented their presence, especially since the troops were there without their permission and because the colonists had to house them and pay for them.

In 1767, a British cabinet member named Charles Townshend convinced Parliament to pass a series of new laws; people called them the Townshend Acts. The Townshend Acts imposed taxes on the colonists for tea, glass, lead, paper, and paint. They also forced the colony of New York to pay for British troops that were stationed there and

allowed British tea merchants to sell their tea in the colonies without paying shipping fees.

The Townshend Acts angered the colonists even more than the Stamp Act. Some reacted by refusing to follow the new laws; some reacted with violent protests.

On March 5, 1770, things came to a head on the streets of Boston, Massachusetts. A mob of angry colonists jeered and threw things at some British soldiers who had been stationed there. In the confusion, the soldiers started firing their muskets. Five colonists died, including a former slave named Crispus Attucks, who became known

as the first American casualty of the war. This incident was later dubbed the Boston Massacre.

In response, Parliament repealed the Townshend Acts—all except for the tax on tea. The British wanted to show the colonists that they were still in charge.

The Boston Tea Party

In 1773, the British passed another new law called the Tea Act. The Tea Act gave one tea company, the East India Company of Britain, the right to export tea into the colonies. This situation, called a monopoly, meant that no other tea companies could ship tea into the colonies; bottom line, the colonists had to buy their tea from the East India Company.

Merchants in port cities like New York City, Charleston, and Philadelphia refused to do business with the East India Company. But Governor Thomas Hutchinson of Massachusetts insisted that the British laws be obeyed. He allowed the East India Company ships to come into Boston Harbor and unload their cargo. He told the colonial merchants that they had to pay taxes on the tea.

A group of sixty or so colonists decided to stage a protest against the Tea Act and the tea tax. On the night of December 16, 1773, they disguised themselves as Native Americans, boarded the East India Company's ships, and dumped 342 chests of tea overboard. This incident was later dubbed the Boston Tea Party.

The British responded by passing yet another new set of laws. The colonists called them the Intolerable Acts because they were so harsh. One of the laws closed the port of Boston until the colonists paid for the 342 chests of ruined tea. Another law replaced Massachusetts's government with a military government, with a British general named Thomas Gage as its governor.

The Intolerable Acts were mostly aimed at Massachusetts, which the British considered to be the center of rebel activity. But the acts helped bring all of the colonies together to stand up against British rule.

The Continental Congress

On September 5, 1774, a group of representatives from twelve of the thirteen colonies gathered in Philadelphia to discuss what to do about the situation with the British. (Georgia was the only colony that did not send representatives.) This group was called the Continental Congress—and later it was called the First Continental Congress because a second group met between 1775 and 1781 for the same purpose. The First Continental Congress had fifty-six delegates, or members. They included George Washington, John Adams, John Jay, Samuel Adams, and Patrick Henry. Each colony had one vote in the decision making.

In September and October, the delegates drew up a declaration of rights to present to the British. These rights included those of life, liberty, assembly, property, and trial by jury. The declaration also stated the colonists' objection to taxation without representation and to British troops being in the colonies without the colonists' permission. The British refused to agree to the Continental Congress's requests and demands, however.

The delegates decided to meet again in May of 1775. But by the time the Second Congress convened, war had broken out between the British and the colonists.

Sons of Liberty

The Sons of Liberty were secret groups of colonists that organized, held meetings, and protested against British rule. The first group came together in Boston in 1765 to oppose the Stamp Act. Other groups formed throughout the colonies. Members included famous patriots such as Paul Revere, Samuel Adams, and John Hancock.

The British Are Coming!

In September of 1774, the first wave of minutemen was organized in Worcester County, Massachusetts. Minutemen were members of militias who could be ready to fight in battle at a "minute's warning." (A militia is an informal group of citizens who defend their community, and the colonies had many of them.)

By this time, many colonists believed that peace was no longer possible between themselves and the British. Other Massachusetts counties and colonies followed suit and assembled their own teams of minutemen.

The British intended to stop the growing colonial rebellion by force, if necessary. In April of 1775, British troops were ordered to go to Lexington, Massachusetts, to arrest Samuel Adams and John Hancock, who were two of the top rebel leaders. After Lexington, the troops were to proceed to the nearby town of Concord and destroy a stockpile of military supplies.

Upon learning this news, minuteman Paul Revere rode his horse through the Massachusetts countryside to warn citizens that the British were coming. He along with fellow riders, William Dawes and Samuel Prescott, were able to warn Samuel Adams and John Hancock in Lexington and the colonists in Concord.

So when the seven hundred or so British troops reached Lexington, they found seventy-seven minutemen and other colonists waiting for them. Shooting broke out, and the British quickly won the battle. They continued to Concord, where they were met by several hundred more armed resisters. There, the British were forced to retreat and head back to Boston.

The Battles of Lexington and Concord marked the official start of the American Revolution.

Patriots Versus Loyalists

Colonists who wanted independence from the British were called patriots. Those who didn't were called loyalists. These terms applied to both soldiers and civilians.

Preparing for War

After the Battles of Lexington and Concord, both sides prepared for war. They recruited more troops, assigned military leaders, and gathered equipment and weapons.

The colonists had serious disadvantages going into the war. First, they did not have a unified or experienced army. Their soldiers were ordinary citizens who may or may not have served in local militias. The men were not used to working together, and they were not used to taking orders from a commander, either.

The lack of unity went even deeper. About a third of the colonial population consisted of loyalists who supported the British king. Some of them even formed units to fight against their fellow colonists.

The colonists had other big problems too. They were not set up to pay, house, or feed their troops during wartime. They lacked money for uniforms, gunpowder, and other supplies. And they didn't have a navy at first, which meant that the British ships could easily attack them from sea.

The British not only had a navy, but they had one of the best armies in the world. They also hired thirty-thousand German soldiers to fight for them.

The odds were definitely against the colonies—at least in the beginning.

Weapons

The most common weapons used in the American Revolution were muskets, rifles, and cannons. Some muskets had bayonets, which were like swords, attached to them.

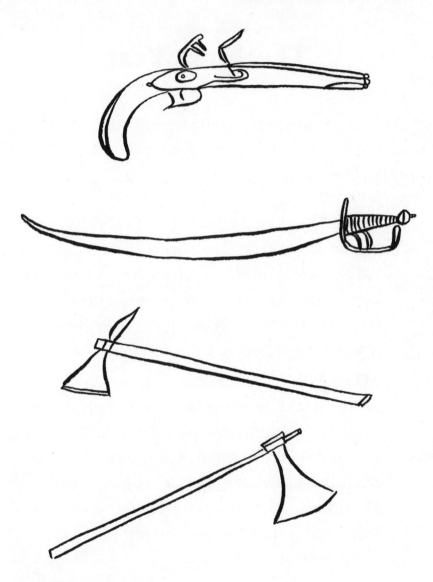

The First Year

Here is a timeline of some important battles and other events during the first year of the war, following the Battles of Lexington and Concord:

- **May 1775:** The Battle of Fort Ticonderoga. Fort Ticonderoga was an important strategic location, on the New York side of Lake Champlain. An American commander named Ethan Allen and his troops (called the Green Mountain Boys) surprised the British soldiers there and took the fort easily, with no casualties.

- **May 1775:** The Continental Congress came together for the second time, again in Philadelphia. It had many of the same members as the First Continental Congress, with the important additions of Benjamin Franklin and Thomas Jefferson. In June, the Second Continental Congress created the Continental Army and named George Washington general and commander in chief.

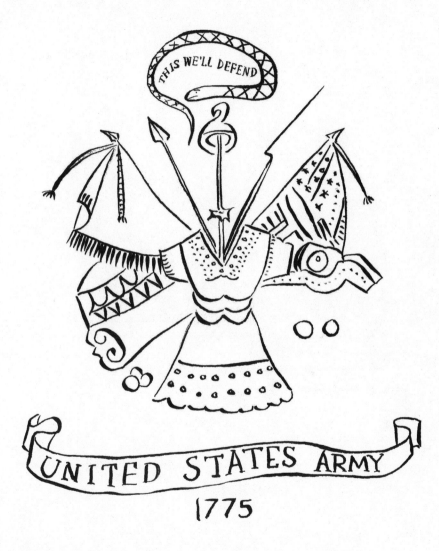

- **June 1775:** The Battle of Bunker Hill. Colonel William Prescott and his troops attacked the British troops in Boston. The British under General William Howe won this battle (which was actually fought on Breed's Hill, not Bunker Hill), although their casualties were high. British troops remained in Boston until March of 1776, when they were driven out by General Washington and his men.

- **November 1775:** The Congress established a Continental Navy.

- **November 1775:** American General Richard Montgomery and his troops captured Montreal, a city in the province of Quebec in Canada. The colonists wanted to control Quebec, which was just north of their border and under British rule, but in December, the British won a battle in Quebec City. Later, the British recaptured Montreal.

- **February 1776:** The Battle of Moore's Creek Bridge. The British were defeated in Moore's Creek, North Carolina. Two months later, North Carolina became the first colony to vote for independence from Britain.

George Washington:
The Early Years

George Washington was born in Virginia in 1732, the son of a wealthy plantation owner and businessman. Washington grew up to be a successful landowner himself as well as a surveyor. (A surveyor is someone who inspects land.) By the age of twenty, he was in charge of Mount Vernon, one of the biggest plantations in the country.

In 1753, Washington was made a major in a militia, launching his long and distinguished military career. He was loyal to the British before he became one of the leaders of the American Revolution.

Washington is sometimes referred to as the "Father of His Country."

The Colonial Soldiers

During the war, most colonial soldiers fell into two categories: militiamen or members of George Washington's Continental Army, which was created in 1775.

Militiamen were farmers, teachers, lawyers, craftspeople, and other ordinary citizens who served part-time to defend their communities. Coming into the war, they had little or no military training. They had to provide their own weapons and even make their own bullets out of lead. Some served in the war only for a few weeks, then left to return home to their jobs and families. Farmers were known to desert their units at harvest time.

In contrast, the men of the Continental Army received military training. They also carried government-issued weapons, and they signed on for longer terms.

In either case, colonial soldiers might be as young as fifteen or sixteen. Some boys were even younger and served as cooks' helpers or drummer boys. (Drum rolls were a way for officers to communicate with their troops, both on and off the battlefield.)

Armies traveled from one area to another depending on where they were needed. In each new place, they had to chop down trees and build their own huts, cabins, and other shelters. At these camps, a dozen soldiers might share one small hut, sleeping in triple bunk beds covered with straw and blankets. Horse- or oxen-drawn wagons brought them food and other supplies.

Uniforms

The American side had little money for uniforms, so the soldiers often wore their own clothes from home. The British soldiers were nicknamed "Redcoats" because their uniform included red coats. The German soldiers wore blue and green coats. American loyalists, fighting for the British, often wore green coats too.

Women in the War

Women served in the war in a number of capacities: as nurses, spies, and even soldiers. Many women also had to defend their homes against enemy soldiers while their husbands and sons were away in battle.

One heroine of the war was Deborah Samson. She disguised herself as a man, called herself "Robert Shurtleff," and served for over a year in the Continental Army. Her true identity was finally discovered when she got sick and ended up in a hospital. She left the army with an "honorable discharge," which means that the military thought she had been a good soldier. Later in her life, she went on to lecture about her experiences in the war. In 1983, she was named a heroine of the Commonwealth of Massachusetts.

Civilian Life

It was difficult for American civilians to lead normal lives during the war. Battles were being fought on their home turf. Patriots raided and stole from the homes of loyalists, and vice versa. Both sides harassed people who were neutral, or didn't take sides.

Most colonists lived on family farms. Despite the war, they had to continue working their land, planting and harvesting. Colonists in the big cities like New York and Philadelphia tried to go on as well, although food shortages and overcrowding became problems as the war dragged on.

Some civilians followed armies from camp to camp, like the wives and children of the soldiers.

The Declaration
of Independence

The colonies had been slowly and gradually separating from Britain for many years. After the first year of war, they were ready to cut their ties completely.

In June of 1776, the Second Continental Congress created a five-member committee to write the document that would become the Declaration of Independence. Thomas Jefferson was one of the committee members and a lead author of the document. The document declared the colonies to be an independent country known as the United States of America. It also listed its many reasons for separating from Great Britain, including taxation without the colonists' consent and limiting their ability to trade with the rest of the world.

The committee presented the document to the Second Continental Congress. The fifty-six delegates discussed the wording and made changes. On July 4, they voted to adopt it.

Even though the document is commonly known as the Declaration of Independence, it does not actually contain that phrase.

John Hancock

In August of 1776, delegates from all the states signed the official copy of the Declaration of Independence. John Hancock, the president of the Second Continental Congress, wrote his name bigger than anyone else's. "John Hancock" later became a nickname for a person's signature.

Five More Years of War

The war went on for five more years after the Declaration of Independence was signed. Here is a timeline of some important battles and other events:

- **June 1776:** The Battle of Valcour Island. General Benedict Arnold and his troops were defeated by British troops on this island in Lake Champlain, but the Americans put up such a good fight that the British retreated to Canada.

- **August 1776:** The Battle of Long Island. British general William Howe showed up in New York Harbor with more than thirty-two thousand troops. After winning this battle against Washington's men, the British went on to occupy New York City in November. Outnumbered, Washington and his troops retreated to New Jersey, then across the Delaware River to Pennsylvania.

- **December 1776 and January 1777:** The Battles of Trenton and Princeton. On Christmas Day, Washington and his men crossed the icy Delaware River and surprised the enemy in Trenton, New Jersey. The Americans won there and in Princeton, New Jersey, against Lord Charles Cornwallis and his men.

- **September and October of 1777:** The Battles of Saratoga. These two battles in Saratoga, New York—the Battle of Freeman's Farm and the Battle of Bemis Heights—were crucial turning points for the Americans. General Horatio Gates and his colonial troops defeated General John Burgoyne and his men, forcing them to formally surrender, return to Britain, and agree never serve in the war again. This victory convinced the French to join the Americans and send much-needed ships, ground troops, and supplies.

- **December 1777 to June 1778:** George Washington and his men encamped at Valley Forge, Pennsylvania, following two defeats in Pennsylvania (at Brandywine and Germantown). The troops were in bad shape due to illness, exhaustion, the harsh winter, hunger, and more. But Washington's leadership as well as the good news from France held them together.

- **December 1778 through the summer of 1780:** British troops captured Savannah, Georgia, and Charleston, South Carolina. By the summer of 1780, the British were in control of much of the South.

- **March 1781:** The Battle of Guilford Courthouse. Washington and his troops defeated Lord Cornwallis and his men in Guilford Courthouse, North Carolina. The British were forced to retreat to Yorktown, Virginia.

- **September to October 1781:** The Battle of Yorktown. Washington had managed to trap Cornwallis's troops in Yorktown, which was on the coast. With the Americans attacking from land and the French navy attacking from the water, Cornwallis was forced to surrender.

Advantage: Americans

The British had gone into the war with many advantages: more money, more equipment, and more and better troops. But as the war wore on, the Americans gained a foothold. They were fighting on their home territory, so they knew the lay of the land. They also gained more soldiers from foreign countries who joined their side. And whenever the British needed to send for more troops or supplies, it meant a three thousand mile journey across the Atlantic.

Benedict Arnold

Benedict Arnold was a general for the colonists—until he secretly switched sides in 1779. In 1780, he was branded a traitor when he tried to hand over West Point, New York, to the British.

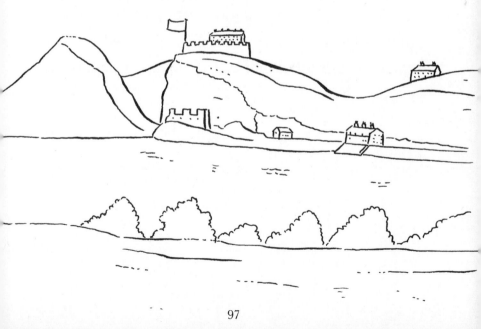

The End of the War

On October 19, 1781, Lord Cornwallis and his British troops surrendered at the Battle of Yorktown. Washington accepted the surrender.

This was the final battle of the American Revolution. Although the fighting had ended, it took several more years for the war to be over. After lengthy negotiations, the two sides signed a peace treaty on September 3, 1783. The treaty, called the Treaty of Paris, acknowledged the United States of America to be an independent country.

The Treaties of Paris

There wasn't just one peace treaty signed on September 3, 1783. Aside from the one between Britain and the United States (the actual "Treaty of Paris"), there was another one between Britain and France, and a third one between Britain and Spain. (Britain and the Netherlands also signed one in May of 1784.)

The Treaty of Paris spelled out the conditions agreed to by the British and the Americans. For example:

- Britain got to keep Canada.

- Both countries would be allowed to navigate the Mississippi River.

- Congress was to recommend to the individual states that American loyalists receive fair treatment.

The Legacy of the War

Now that the United States of America was officially its own country, it needed a new constitution. A constitution was necessary to create a new and lasting federal government and to spell out its duties and powers.

The Second Continental Congress had actually created an earlier constitution, called the Articles of Confederation, in 1776 and 1777. But the document, which was ratified, or made official, in 1781, was full of problems. Among other things, it didn't give the federal government enough power.

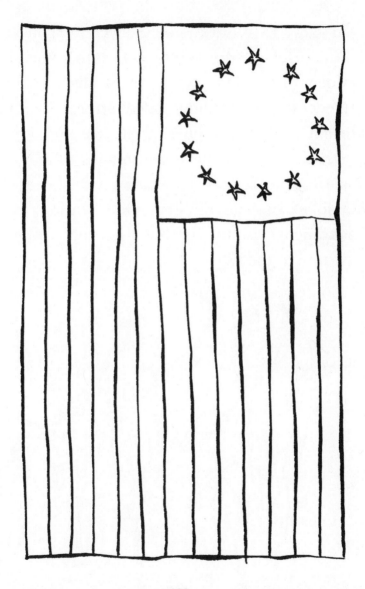

In 1787, a Constitutional Convention convened in Philadelphia, with George Washington as their president. Their aim was to revise the Articles of Confederation, but they ended up starting from scratch. In September of that year, the group approved the new document called the Constitution. It was ratified by the states over the following year. The Constitution, with amendments, is still the basis for the American government today.

A new American government took shape in accordance with the Constitution. In March of 1789, the first United States Congress convened. The following month, George Washington was elected to be the first president of the United States.

The United States was finally and truly independent. But with independence came a whole new set of problems. The states often clashed with each other and with the federal government, especially over slavery. These and other issues would come to a head in 1861 with the Civil War.

Well, it's been a great adventure. Good-bye, American Revolution!

Where to next?

Also available:

Coming in August 2016!

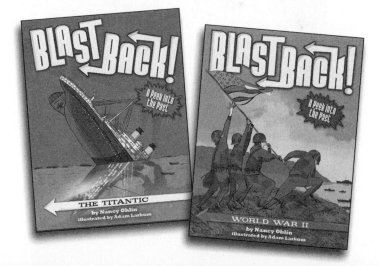

Selected Bibliography

The American Revolution by David F. Burg, Facts on File, 2001

DK Eyewitness Books: American Revolution by Stuart Murray, DK Publishing, 2000

Encyclopedia Britannica Online, www.britannica.com

Encyclopedia Britannica Kids Online, www.kids.britannica.com

Patriots in Petticoats: Heroines of the American Revolution by Shirley Raye Redmond, Random House, 2004

A Revolutionary War Timeline by Elizabeth Raum, Capstone Press, 2014

NANCY OHLIN is the author of the YA novels *Always, Forever* and *Beauty* as well as the early chapter book series Greetings from Somewhere under the pseudonym Harper Paris. She lives in Ithaca, New York, with her husband, their two kids, two cats, a bunny, and assorted animals who happen to show up at their door. Visit her online at nancyohlin.com.

ADAM LARKUM is a freelance illustrator based in the United Kingdom. In his fifteen years of illustrating, he's worked on over forty books. In addition to his illustration work, he also dabbles in animation and develops characters for television.